Scott R Bullard

Guide to Wachusett Mountain with Accompanying Map

Scott R Bullard

Guide to Wachusett Mountain with Accompanying Map

ISBN/EAN: 9783337290153

Printed in Europe, USA, Canada, Australia, Japan

Cover: Foto ©Lupo / pixelio.de

More available books at **www.hansebooks.com**

TO

Wachusett Mountain,

WITH

Accompanying Map.

COMPILED AND PUBLISHED BY

S. C. & M. H. BULLARD.

PRINCETON, MASS.

1872.

SNOW BROTHERS,

Printers,

WORCESTER, MASS.

PREFACE.

IN compiling a Guide for Wachusett Mountain, the author has endeavored to supply a need already urgent, and which each season grows more pressing as the number of its visitors increases. Already their annual number far exceeds 10,000.

There is something so strange and foreign to nearly all visitors in a birdseye view from the mountain top, that they become somewhat confused, and for want of a reliable guide lose much of the pleasure and profit of a visit. Many of the mountains, villages and other objects of interest they have no name for, while others are incorrectly named.

The writer, familiar from boyhood with Wachusett and the topography of its surroundings, and whose later opportunities for correct observation of most of the territory it overlooks have been equaled by few, was surprised to find, in taking observations for the accompanying map, how much he had both to learn and to unlearn.

In compiling the accompanying map we have taken Wachusett as a centre, giving a circle of 45 miles radius This gives a circle of 90 miles in diameter, containing the larger part of Massachusetts and portions of the four bordering states.

We have placed no village on the map not wholly or partially visible from Wachusett, hence several large villages near by are omitted.

In New England it is usual to call all our inland bodies of water *ponds*, except the very largest, while outside of New England, both in our own and other countries, the natural sheets of water are called *lakes*, the artificial, *ponds*. We have adopted the more universal name, partly because the distinction is familiar to a large portion of our visitors, but mainly because we can thereby furnish a more correct Guide; for some of our large reservoirs which are in full tide in June, are shorn of their fair proportions in August and September.

Some of the mountains in New Hampshire have been much christened. Some have two and some three local names. We have adopted those used by the New Hampshire State Survey.

The writer would acknowledge his deep obligations to Prof. Quimby of the New Hampshire State Survey, for his valuable assistance, and also to his other friends who have kindly aided him in his undertaking.

S. C. B.

Mount Wachusett.

IDWAY between Massachusetts Bay and the Connecticut River a belt of broken hill country extends across the Old Bay State, whose higher peaks rise to the dignity of mountains.

Of these mountain peaks WACHUSETT is the crowning eminence. In height above the level of the sea second only to Greylock or Saddle Mountain, it far surpasses its loftier sister in the beauty and extent of its scenery.

Most of our higher mountains are hemmed in by ridges of less magnitude, but which are still high enough to intercept the view beyond. Wachusett, on the contrary, is environed by and overlooks detached hills, which detract little and add much to the scenery. Nearly all of our mountain districts are newly and sparsely settled ; the land but little cultivated and the roads rough. This usual rule is also reversed in the case of the country around Wachusett.

Nearly two centuries ago, in spite of its rough and rocky hills, the Puritan settlers were attracted by its fertile soil, and their thrifty descendants now till a highly cultivated country and form an opulent community.

The roads for so hilly a country are unusually good ; they abound in fine prospects and charming landscapes. The valleys are dotted here and there with picturesque lakes and ponds ; the mountain streams as they course along the meadows or tumble down the glens, turn many a wheel of industry ; while railroads stretch along the valleys and wind among the hills.

Wachusett is situated in the northerly part of Princeton, sixteen miles northwest of Worcester, ten southwest of Fitchburg and forty-eight a little north of west from Boston. Its height above the sea level has been the subject of much dispute. There was a wide discrepancy between the earlier barometrical observations, which varied from 2018 to 3000 feet. When Wachusett was occupied as a coast survey station in 1860, its true altitude was found to be between the two extremes, or 2480 feet. Being the nearest to the coast of our high mountains, it is often the first land seen from vessels approaching Boston Harbor.

Wachusett was a famous Indian resort. Their camping ground and rendezvous was on the northeast side, around a large, flat-topped rock near the margin of Wachusett Lake, a beautiful sheet of water which nestles close to the side of its parent mountain. Here their council fires were lighted. expeditions planned, and treaties made : and here Mrs. Rowlandson, the white woman taken captive at Lancaster during King Philip's War, was finally ransomed.

There are three ways of ascending Wachusett. One from the north by way of Bolton's ; a second on the east side, from Pine Hill by way of the Pine Hill House ; a third is by the Coast Survey Road from the Mountain House on the southeast side. This, the most accessible route, is adopted by more than nine-tenths of the visitors. At the Mountain House the carriage road ends, but there is a well beaten track and practicable cart road to the summit, a little less than a mile distant.

In ascending from the Mountain House, we are already over 1200 feet above the level of the sea, or nearly half the altitude of Wachusett, and here we have a very commanding view, which will widen out as we ascend higher. Passing upward a somewhat steep path, we soon enter a pasture whose rocky hillsides abound with ferns, some of which are rare and beautiful. Here, too, thrive many sturdy old sugar maples, whose cooling shade is quite welcome in summer. That offshoot of Wachusett which branches out to the east, a little to the north of us, whose head is crested with forest, is Pine Hill, while Little Wachusett,

an equally high but bare hill, raises its head a
mile to the south.

Until we reach the forest, which is one-third
of the way up, the path has a northwest
course. Here we turn a right angle, taking a
northeast course over the steepest part of the
route. Reaching a comparatively level spot,
the road turns sharply to the west, then to the
southwest, passing over a spur of the mountain, so that we reach the summit from the
southwesterly side. This winding path gives
the weary pedestrian an opportunity to enjoy
some fine wayside views.

Perhaps the first impression the visitor re-
ceives on arriving at the summit, is wonder
that in so thickly settled a community there
should be so much forest or waste land. If
that is the *first* impression, we may be pretty
sure the *second* will be wonder that there is
not more ; so irregular, hilly, and unlevel is
the country below. Save where some placid
lake gleams in the sun, we see not one square
foot of level surface, but instead, the whole
panorama seems a jumble of hills and valleys,
fields and forests, lakes and villages, strangely
mixed together.

The view, too, is so little interrupted by surrounding hills, that it extends over portions of
six states.

It has been claimed that from Wachusett
three hundred villages and cities could be

seen. In taking observations for the map, the author intended to test the truth of this assertion. but the great labor and expense involved —quite out of proportion to the utility and value of the object,—compelled him to give up the undertaking.

Toward the south, the fact that we are looking toward the sun and consequently toward the shaded side. renders it difficult to discern any except prominent villages. Toward the west, in the Connecticut Valley, nearly all the distant villages are screened by the belt of high ground about twenty-five miles distant. To the north, the mountain ridges of New Hampshire, except in occasional vistas, also intercept the vision. But to the northeast, the east and southeast, within an angle extending from Dover, N. H., to Bridgewater, Mass., the great majority of villages from the interior to the seacoast are often to be seen.

Here we would remark that comparatively small, distant objects, like villages, are made much more distinct and prominent when the sun is at our backs and consequently lights up the side nearest us. Most of the distant villages are only visible when thus illuminated.

Hence points of interest toward the east are best seen when lighted up by the rays of the declining sun.

Often, in the afternoon of a clear, cool day,

the eastern horizon seems, to the naked eye, quite dotted over with villages. Many of these, which to the unassisted eye seem but a single village, are resolved by the telescope into several, some more remote than others. But the difficulty even an experienced eye finds in identifying the more distant villages is so great, that we have omitted on the map those of lesser prominence, as tending to confuse and fatigue the casual visitor.

It is unfortunate that the great majority of the visitors to Wachusett come only in the hottest months, when haze and smoke most abound. If they would come in May or early June, or better still, when the frosts have cleared the atmosphere in Autumn, that "crowning glory of the year," they would be repaid by a view far more magnificent than that of July or August.

On the highest point of Wachusett stands the Summit House, built and kept by Mr. Morse. This is crowned with an observatory which affords the finest views of the country below, and with his telescope and field glasses, is a great convenience to visitors.

Descriptive Guide.

As we glance around us from the summit, we find the most conspicuous object to be a large mountain toward the northeast called the Grand Monadnock. As this prominent point can almost always be seen, we will take it as our starting point, and passing to the right, point out most of the noticeable objects below. It is called the "Grand Monadnock" because there are three "Monadnocks," of which this is the central and much the largest. It is a little north of northwest, and is a grim looking pile with sharply defined outlines, the peak being composed of bare precipitous rocks. Monadnock is said in the Indian Language to signify a "Peak of Rocks."

From the northern base of Monadnock a ridge stretches off to the northeast, sinking nearly into the horizon as it reaches the Ipswich Group. Near the eastern extremity of this ridge the crest of a distant mountain rises like a haycock above it. This is Sunapee, sixty miles distant. Toward Monadnock and four miles from us is Westminster, on the northeast margin of a fine sheet of water

called Meetinghouse Lake. Seven miles farther
to the north is the village of Ashburnham, so
shaded with trees we can see but little of it
but its steeples, thus forming a contrast to its
thriving sister, Winchendon, whose spires are
not visible, but whose new-built streets are
rising into notice. Beyond the New Hampshire line may be seen Rindge and Jaffrey, the
latter almost in the shadow of Monadnock.

Passing eastward to where the Monadnock
Ridge ends we find a cluster of mountains
called the New Ipswich Group. The nearest
and one of the most western is the Great Wa-
tatic, a round, steep mount, nearly covered
with evergreens. A little to the North is a
long, smooth ridge called Mt. Barrett. A
little to the east of Barrett is another conical
hill called Mt. Whittemore. North of the last
another ridge. Mt. Kidder, trends to the
northeast, while Temple Mountain, like a
heartless rival, plants itself just beyond, overlooks and outflanks it, then saucily sweeping
down into the valley to the northeast it joins
hands and connects with Pack Monadnock,
the mountain ridge to the northeast.

A little west of the lowest depression between Temple Mountain and Pack Monadnock you may see the conical head of a mountain loom up. This peak is the more notic-
able because here in one line we can see two
of New Hampshire's more noted mountains.

These are Kearsarge, seventy miles, and Moosillauke, one hundred and twenty miles distant. Kearsarge has already become famous in our annals, from the gallantry of its namesake in our navy, which fought and sank that scourge of the seas, the rebel Alabama. So exactly does the more lofty and distant Moosillauke stand behind his warlike sister, that at best his crest appears like a thin veil above the fearless Kearsarge.

We have spoken of the Pack Monadnock, the mountain we see to the northeast of Temple and Kidder. The origin of 'its curious name is somewhat shrouded in doubt. Not that there is no account of it handed down, but that there are several different ones. All agree that it dates back to the time anterior to roads, when paths and pack horses were the means by which the early settlers conveyed their goods and chattels from the settlements to their forest homes. Whether the contour of the mountain had any striking resemblance to a packed horse, or whether a pack was here lost or one found, the reader has at least a choice of traditions.

Some distance to the east of Pack Monadnock we see two mountains side by side. These are the Uncanoomocs or Twin Mountains. A little farther to the west you see a single mountain called Lyndeboro Mountain. Towards this last mountain the ridge from

Wachusett House,

PRINCETON, MASS.

———◆———

THIS HOUSE, PLEASANTLY LOCATED AT PRINCE-
TON CENTRE, OFFERS EXTRA ACCOMMODA-
TIONS TO

Permanent and Transient Guests.

———

Stages leave this House, connecting with every
Train on the

Boston, Barre & Gardner R. R.

———

P. A. BEAMAN & SON,

Proprietors.

Pack Monadnock slopes off to the northeast, till it terminates in a moderate sized mound midway between the two mountains. That mound is Pinnacle Mountain, and it stands in the direct line to the White Mountains one hundred and forty miles distant. In a clear day Mt. Washington may be seen directly behind Pinnacle, with its summit a little to the right and considerably higher, while clustering thick around it like a bodyguard, mainly a little to the west, are the shadowy forms of his companion peaks.

On the eastern side of Lyndeboro Mountain, and partially behind, we see the blue outline of a larger and more distant mountain. That is Gunstock, seventy-six miles distant, standing on the border of Lake Winnipiseogee. A little to the east of Gunstock and just west of the most western of the Twin Mountains is Catamount Mountain, of considerable magnitude, sixty-five miles distant.

Looking out from Wachusett a little north of northeast, towards Lyndeboro, we see a long, narrow pond, which at the farther end turns sharply to the left, forming an L.

This is the Reservoir pond of Wymansville, a few houses of which can be seen near the end of the L. Beyond we see the villages of Crockerville and Wachusett, while a little more to the left and more than twenty miles distant, we see Mason, N. H. Beyond Wa-

Mountain House,

Princeton, Mass.

Situated on the side of WACHUSETT MOUNTAIN, 1200 feet above the level of the sea.   Affording

Extensive Views. Cool and bracing Mountain Air.

Open for Boarders and Transient Guests

FROM JUNE 1st, TO NOVEMBER 1st.

Livery   Stable,   Bowling   Alleys,   and   Croquet Grounds Attached.

———

☞ Schools, Excursions and Picnic Parties from a distance, desiring to visit Wachusett and return same day can make arrangements to come by R. R. at reduced fare.

SEND FOR CIRCULAR.

———

M. H. BULLARD,

PROPRIETOR.

chusett village, and nine miles from here, the
winding valley that seems lined with villages,
turns behind a hill with a curious ragged grey
head, while a considerable cluster of houses
nestles to its side on the left, and apparently
a still larger village crops out on its right
That hill is Rollstone, and its ragged grey
poll shows where it has been literally scalped
by the granite quarrymen, while the village on
the left is part of Fitchburg, that on the right
South Fitchburg.   A little to the left of Fitchburg, and more than thirty miles distant, may
be seen Amherst, N. H.

About six miles to the east and a little to the
right of Rollstone may be seen, on rising
ground, the village of Lunenburg, which rejoices in the posssession of two pretty lakes
one near the village, the other three miles to
the south.   Passing beyond the low range o
Lunenburg Hills to the Townsend Valley, we
notice a chain of villages running northwes
and southeast.   Here are Groton, West Gro
ton, Townsend Harbor, Townsend and Wes
Townsend, while a few miles beyond are Pep
perell and Dunstable, and farther still may b
seen Hollis and Nashua.

Returning to our starting place and lookin
east, we see a long, narrow pond stretchin
north and south close to the foot of the moun
tain.   This is Paradise Pond, and its nam
may mislead, for it is not the most favored o

our ponds. The little Rocky Lake that we
see two miles beyond, almost hidden in the
dense forest, far excels it in beanty. The
large irregular sheet of water that we see six
miles away to the northeast is a reservoir.

The long, high hill a little south of this reservoir, whose forest clad sides are darkly tint-
ed with evergreens, is Wanoosnoc Hill, and
the beautiful village to the right and just beyond, which seems fairly embosomed with
hills, is Leominster. Beyond Leominster
we may see in succession Ayer, Lyttleton,
Chelmsford and Lowell, and beyond, with a
fine, clear afternoon and a good telescope,
most of the villages in Essex and Rocking-
ham Counties. Ten miles farther, and a little
to the south of Leominster, may be seen on
high ground, the villages of Still River and
Harvard, and beyond those Acton, South
Acton and Carlisle.

Returning and taking another new departure, the awkward looking village that we see
straggling around the edge of a ravine, three
miles to the southeast of us, is East Princeton,
the sheet of water we see a little east of it is
Stewart's Pond, and the high hill to the left o
it is Justice Hill. The village of Sterling is
quite hidden by Fitch Hill, but turning east
ward twelve miles to the Nashua Valley we
see another chain of villages; North Lancas
ter, Lancaster, South Lancaster and the large

Vermont & Massachusetts
RAILROAD.

EXCURSION

VIA.

HOOSAC TUNNEL RAILROAD LINE.

ON AND AFTER JULY 1, 1872,

ickets by this favorite route will be issued to Hoosac Tunnel, North Adams, Troy, Albany, Saratoga, Niagara Falls, and re-urn, at REDUCED RATES. Also,

ROUND TRIP TICKETS,

tood for 30 days, and can be used either way, via Hoosac Tunel, Troy, Saratoga, Niagara Falls, Albany, New York, and Newport.

The above tickets are for sale at the Fitchburg Railroad depot nd at 69 Washington Street. Also at the principal railroad of-ces in Boston and vicinity, and all Stations on Vermont and Iassachusetts R. R.

Passengers leaving Boston by morning train ar-ive at Saratoga at 6.25 P. M.; also make close onnections at Troy with N. Y. Central Express or Buffalo and Niagara Falls, at 4.45 P. M.

Cars leave Fitchburg Railroad depot at 7.30 and 11 A. M., iardner at 9.57 A. M., and 2.05 P. M.

For further information inquire at the office of the line, *9 Washington Street, Boston.*

O. T. RUGGLES, Gen. Agent,
FITCHBURG, MASS.

and showy village of Clinton.   Beyond Lancaster, may be seen Bolton, Stowe, Hudson and Concord; and the long, high ridge we see beyond, which forms one of our eastern landmarks, is Prospect Hill, in Waltham.   Prospect Hill, or Mt. Prospect as it is sometimes called, is almost in the direct line to Boston, and to a certain extent intercepts the view, but the loftier objects, and South Boston, Charlestown and the villages north and south are, in tolerably clear weather, visible.   The chimneys of South Boston, that of the Navy Yard, and even ships under full sail are easily seen.   Not so with Bunker Hill Monument. Its tint is so nearly that of the ocean beyond, that it can rarely be seen except when it glistens in the sun.

Over South Lancaster may be seen, in the blue distance, a regular moundlike hill. This, the Blue Hill of Milton. fifty-five miles distant, is another of the seaboard landmarks, and except in hazy weather can almost always be seen.   In quite clear weather the villages about Blue Hill and many far beyond and south of it are plainly visible.

Beyond Clinton we see West Berlin and Berlin, while quite above them sits Marlboro, a city on a hill.   Perhaps I should say a city on two hills, for literally there seems to be a wide gulf between the two wings.   These two villages of Marlboro have settled down togeth-

BOSTON, BARRE & GARDNER

Railroad Company.

On and after MONDAY, JUNE 17th, 1872, trains will

LEAVE BOSTON, (corner of Beach and Albany Streets)

FOR

WORCESTER, GARDNER AND WAY STATIONS, 5 A.M.
(way), 7 A. M. (way), 8.30 A. M.(express), 9 A. M. (express),
1.30 P. M. (way), 3 P. M. (express), 4.30 P. M. (way).

LEAVE WORCESTER FOR

HOLDEN, PRINCETON, HUBBARDSTON, and GARDNER
8.30 A. M. 12 35, 4.45, 6.30 P. M.

LEAVE GARDNER FOR

HUBBARDSTON, PRINCETON, HOLDEN, WORCESTER
and BOSTON, 5.35, 8.15. 11.45 A. M. 4.15 P. M.

LEAVE WORCESTER FOR

BOSTON, 7 A. M. (way) 9.45 A. M. (way), 1.40 P. M. (way), 3.25
P. M. (express), 6 P M. (way)

Stages leave Holden, Princeton, Hubbardston and Gardner
from all trains.

CONNECTIONS.

AT GARDNER with all trains on Vermont & Massachusetts
Railroad, to and from Hoosac Tunnel, Greenfield. Brattleboro', &c.

AT WORCESTER, with Worcester and Nashua, Boston &
Albany, Providence & Worcester, and Norwich & Worcester Railroads, and

EXPRESS FRIEGHT TRAINS

to New York, via Providence or Norwich.

T. B. SARGEANT, Sup't.

er in so friendly a manner we trust they ar
not rivals, and that they do not, like som
neighbors, scold across the way. A little be
yond and to the right of Marlboro may b
seen a small village with a single prominer
church. This is Southboro, while beyond an
a little farther to the right is Ashland.

The two lakes that add so much to the land
scape, eight miles away to the southeast, ar
the Washacum Lakes, in Sterling.

Sterling Junction, a railroad station, an
noted for its annual Camp-meetings, is clos
by on the right, but quite screened by th
woods. The valley, a little farther to th
right, down which we look and where we oc
casionally get glimpses of ponds of water, i
the valley of the South Branch of the Nashua
and the two cosy villages we see in it are Oak
dale and West Boylston. As the valley me
anders around West Boylston to the east an
northeast, we see beyond it, and to the left o
West Boylston, a small but conspicuous vil
lage. This is Boylston. To the right, an
five miles beyond, is Northboro', while betwee
the last two villages, but far beyond, may b
discerned the spires of Westboro' and Ho
liston. Almost directly over Boylston, bu
fifteen miles beyond, glistens in the sun, Hop
kinton, another "City on a Hill."

Some distance to the right of Boylstor
peering above a tract of woodland, is the vi
lage of Shrewsbury, while as much farther t

American House,

Opposite the Depots,

FITCHBURG, = MASS.

VM. F. DAY & CO., - Proprietors.

Free Carriage to and from the depots.

WM. F. DAY.   ALONZO BURT.

JOEL BROTHERS,

MANUFACTURERS AND DEALERS IN

Choice Cigars,

Smoking and Chewing Tobacco, Pipes, &c.

No. 1 American House Block and 160 Main Street,

FITCHBURG, - - - MASS.

OEL JOEL.   REUBEN JOEL.

the right but considerably beyond, stands
Grafton, another large and showy hill village.
A little to the west of Grafton may be seen
New England Village, while quite beyond we
may see several villages as we look down the
Blackstone Valley.

Glancing farther to the right, and about
sixteen miles distant, the straggling, but quite
picturesque city that we see, is Worcester.
Twenty-five years ago Worcester was repre-
sented on Wachusett only by two or three
church spires, and by the College of the Holy
Cross and was difficult to point out.   Even
now few public buildings can be seen.   But so
many of her handsome suburban streets have
scaled the surrounding hills that she already
sits in the landscape like a Queen in the
South.

Returning to our starting point and looking
toward the south, the high bare hill we see,
one and a half miles distant, is Little Wachusett.   From this eminence a high ridge sweeps
out, with an occasional depression, several
miles south.   Its highest point almost conceals
the beautiful village of Princeton, two and a
half miles distant.

Seven miles beyond Princeton, in the midst
of an expanse of comparatively level country
so clothed with wood that it looks like an im-
mense forest, are seen the two spires of the
village of Holden.   This quiet, staid village of
Holden, which to the visitor on Wachusett, al-

Summit House,

SITUATED ON

The Top of Wachusett Mountain.

AN OBSERVATORY is connected with the House, affording the finest views of the country around Wachusett.

Meals at all Hours.

And Lodging for a limited number.

Accommodations for Picnic Parties Furnished.

· WM. G. MORSE, Proprietor.

S. M. & E. B. DOLE,

Livery Stable.

Arrangements may be made by mail or otherwise for conveying Excursionists. Picnic Parties and Schools from the railroad to Wachusett Mountain or other points in the vicinity.

West Street, - - Fitchburg, Mass.

ways looked as if it had never been able to get out of the woods, under the stimulus of railroad facilities seems to be taking a new departure.

A little to the west of Princeton, and five miles exactly south from us, we see a pretty sheet of water—Quinnipoxet Lake. Beyond this and just in front of another sheet of water, is Eagleville. Still keeping due south, we notice a smooth, bare hill, the loftiest eminence in that direction, called Asnebumskit. Just over the western edge of this hill, a single prominent church spire represents the village of Leicester. Far beyond, several villages in Connecticut are sometimes visible, but as we see them on the shaded side, they can rarely be identified.

The village a little to the northwest of Asnebumskit is Paxton, and that nearly over Paxton and fifteen miles beyond, is Charlton. A little to the northwest of Paxton is a high, abrupt, wood covered hill, called Turkey Hill, and just to the right of that and beyond, is Spencer. Looking farther to the right, and about nine miles distant, we see Rutland, a small village perched upon a high hill, and still farther to the west, and six miles beyond, is another small village, Oakham. Between these last two villages, and farther away, is seen the larger village of North Brookfield. Beyond, and a little to the right of Oakham,

PROSPECT HOUSE,

Princeton Centre, Mass.

This house is delightfully located at the centre of the Town, and

Open through the Summer Season to Permanent and Transient Guests.

Stages leave the house, connecting with all trains on Boston, Barre and Gardner R. R.

I. F. THOMPSON, PROPRIETOR.

KEENE HARNESS.

JOHN CARPENTER,

MANUFACTURER OF AND DEALER IN

Light and Heavy Harnesses,

Robes, Blankets, Whips, Fly Nets, Trunks, Valises, Brushes, Combs, Neats Foot Oil, &c., constantly on hand.

Harnesses Neatly Repaired and Oiled.

Clark's Block, Head of Central Square,

KEENE, - N. H.

and almost exactly southwest of where we stand, is New Braintree.

Looking beyond, and a little to the west of New Braintree, we see a high hill in the town of Hardwick, called Mt. McDougal, while a little to the left of McDougal, looking through a depression between the hills, is seen Ware Mountain, an offshoot of the Holyoke range.

Turning back, and still farther to the west, we come to Barre, twelve miles distant, a large village, on a high hill. Barre is not singular in that respect. The early settlers to the southwest and west of us were evidently a hardy and highminded people ; men who feared neither bleak winds nor drifting snows, and who disdained to plant their villages in valleys so long as commanding eminences could be found. Thanks to that peculiarity of theirs for adding much to the beauty of the scenery.

Over Barre lies Mt. Holyoke and Mt. Tom, but their crests do not rise sufficiently above the intervening hills to distinctly point them out. Half way from us to Barre, but a little to the south, we see glimpses of Asneconcomick Lake. This is the largest of the lakes in the vicinity and yields to none in beauty.

A little to the north of this last lake, Moosehorn, forms a still more prominent feature in the landscape, while a little to the left of Moosehorn, in the distance may be seen the villages of Dana and Prescott.

Three miles to the west of Moosehorn, on

high ground, is the village of Hubbardston.
A little to the north of Hubbardston, almost
due west, fifteen miles distant, is the village of
Petersham.   A little to the north of Petersham and beyond, is New Salem, and still beyond and to the northward is the village of
Wendell.   Over Wendell may be seen Greylock or Saddle Mountain, the highest summit
in the State, eighty miles distant.   Greylock
is beyond the Hoosac Range, almost the highest peak of which is overlooked by its dome-
like head.

As the eye sweeps north over the Hoosac
range, it here meets with a considerable elevation, which ends about five degrees farther
north in a sudden depression or gap.   Greylock lifts its conical crest just south of the
centre of this elevation and is in the exact
line of the Hoosac Tunnel.

Taking a new departure, the sheet of water
we see at the foot of the mountain on the west
is Whitney's Pond, while the village, twelve
miles farther on, that we see rising above a
wood northeast of Petersham, is Phillipston.
Somewhat nearer and a little to the right of
Phillipston, and directly over a pond five
miles distant, is Templeton, while a mile and
a half east of the last village is East Templeton.   Looking upward to the horizon from between these two villages we may see Mt.
Grace, thirty miles distant.   A little to the
right of East Templeton, looking down the

VINUM CALISAYÆ ET FERRI.

Relief For The Suffering.

FAIRBANKS & PIPER'S
WINE

o f

CALISAYA (PERUVIAN) BARK,

AND

IRON.

The Most Reliable Iron Tonic Known.

CURES Dyspepsia.
CURES Debility
CURES Lassitude.
CURES Languor.
CURES Depression of Spirits.
CURES Weakness.
CURES Want of Energy.
CURES Loss of Appetite.
CURES Imperfect Circulation of Blood.
CURES Cold Extremities.

And in short it

CURES a multitude of disorders arising from a weak state of the blood, or an impaired state of the digestive organs.

PREPARED AND SOLD BY

FAIRBANKS & PIPER, Druggists,

No. 10 Front Street,

WORCESTER, - - - - - - MASS.

Ask your Druggist for it and take nothing else.

valley of Otter River, we see in the order of
distance, Jonesville and Baldwinsville.   Rais-
ing our eyes from this last village, about
thirty-five miles distant we see Rattlesnake·
Mountain, and lifting them higher still to the
Green Mountain Range, we notice one. of its
more important peaks, Mt. Stratton.   Turning again to the right, and just to the right of
a pond eight miles distant, we see the village
of South Gardner, and a little to the right of
that is Gardner.   Looking over Gardner, thirty miles distant we may see Little Monadnock.
A little to the right of this mountain, and
somewhat nearer, is the village of Fitzwilliam,
and to the right of that is an abrupt rocky
ridge, a continuation of Grand Monadnock,
which rejoices in the name of Gap Mountain.

We have now passed around the circle to
our starting place, the Grand Monadnock.

In our description we have passed lightly
over the distant villages because for the Tourist they may be quite as readily located by
reference to the map.   Our plan has been to
point out the prominent points in the environs.
Should any visitor wish a closer inspection of
any part of the field, we trust the landmarks
we have given will materially aid him in the
analysis.

Routes for Reaching Wachusett.

There are several railroad routes which will bring the tourist to the near vicinity of Wachusett.

The Boston, Barre and Gardner Railroad, connecting Worcester with Gardner, passes through Princeton. Stages connect with the several trains at Princeton Station for Princeton and the Mountain House, four miles distant. At Worcester this Road connects with all the roads centering there, and at Gardner with the Vermont & Mass. R. R. for Greenfield, Brattleboro' and Hoosac Tunnel.

The Worcester & Nashua R. R., connecting Worcester with central New Hampshire, passes to the east. Its station for the Mountain House is Oakdale, nine miles distant, where private conveyance can be obtained.

The Boston, Clinton & Fitchburg R. R. connects Fitchburg and the railroads centering there with Boston, Taunton, New Bedford, and Providence. Tourists and excursion parties taken by private conveyance to Wachusett Mountain over the favorite Forest Road from Leominster or Fitchburg stations, nine miles distant.

The Vermont and Massachusetts R. R., connecting Boston and Fitchburg with the Connecticut Valley, passes six miles to the northeast.   Passengers from the east can take private conveyance from Wachusett Station, six miles distant.   Passengers from the West can take Boston, Barre & Gardner R. R. at Gardner for Princeton.

ROUTES BY PUBLIC ROADS.

Where one can conveniently do so, unquestionably the most delightful way of taking a trip to Wachusett and its environs, is by one's own conveyance. Massachusetts surpasses all her sister states in the excellence of her public roads. Even in the broken hill country the traveller finds the highways unusually good, while the great variety in the landscape affords many beautiful and picturesque views.

Either route you take from the seaboard takes one through several delightful and thrifty villages, and among the hills and valleys the roadside teems with an unusual variety of trees, shrubs, flowers and ferns. As one ascends to the high ground the air grows more bracing and the heat less oppressive. At the Mountain House the mercury in the thermometer rarely rises as high as 84 degrees, and even then the mountain breeze which stirs at nightfall, almost always renders a thick coat desirable.

To residents of Essex and the Northern
part of Middlesex Counties, a pleasant route
is via Groton and Fitchburg.   This is a very
pleasant route ; and if the traveller wishes to
stop by the way at Fitchburg, he will find ex-
cellent hotel accommodations at the American
House.

North of Boston a good route is via Concord and Lancaster, twelve miles from Wachusett Mountain, where there is a good hotel
for those who do not wish to drive through in
one day.

South of Boston another route is via Fram-
ingham, and either Marlboro or Northboro to
Clinton, twelve miles from the Mountain,where
a good hotel is kept.

From Providence and the vicinity the short-
est and easiest route is via the Blackstone
Valley and Worcester, sixteen miles distant.

ADVERTISERS' INDEX.

www.ingramcontent.com/pod-product-compliance
Lightning Source LLC
Chambersburg PA
CBHW021442090426
42739CB00009B/1603